This book belongs to

Fair Dinkum AUSSIE EASTER

Colin Buchanan • John McIntosh

SCHOLASTIC

SYDNEY AUCKLAND NEW YORK TORONTO LONDON MEXICO CITY
NEW DELHI HONG KONG BUENOS AIRES PUERTO RICO

Dedicated to Australia's infants and primary school teachers, especially the ones who taught me all those years ago. Treasure the privilege, endure the hard yards, keep finding things to chuckle at and may you be rewarded with sweet glimpses into the gift you give to the precious children in your care. C.B.

Scholastic Australia
ABN 11 000 614 577
PO Box 579
Gosford NSW 2250
www.scholastic.com.au

Part of the Scholastic Group
Sydney · Auckland · New York · Toronto · London · Mexico City
· New Delhi · Hong Kong · Buenos Aires · Puerto Rico

Published by Scholastic Australia in 2009.
Words by Colin Buchanan © 2007 Universal Music Publishing Australia P/L.
Illustrations copyright © John McIntosh 2009.
Graphic design by Stewart Yule, Darkroom Door.

National Library of Australia Cataloguing-in-Publication entry:
Author: Buchanan, Colin, 1964-
Title: Fair Dinkum Aussie Easter / Colin Buchanan; illustrator, John McIntosh
ISBN: 978-1-74169-234-1 (hbk.)
Target Audience: For children.
Dewey Number: 781.520994

Typset in Lomba Book.

Printed by Tien Wah Press, Malaysia.

10 9 8 7 6 5 4 3 2 1   9 / 0 1 2 3

Fair Dinkum AUSSIE EASTER

Contents

Aussie Easter Oi! Oi! Oi!   4

The Easter Long Weekend   6

When it's Easter in Australia   10

Little Barry Bilby   12

The Easter Hat Parade   14

The Great Big Aussie Easter Egg Hunt   16

Australians All Love Hot Cross Buns   20

The Easter Bunny Got the Sack   22

Aussie Easter Oi! Oi! Oi!

Chorus
Aussie Easter Oi! Oi! Oi!
Aussie Easter Oi! Oi! Oi!
Aussie Oi!
Easter Oi!
Aussie Easter Oi! Oi! Oi!

Melted eggs in the back of the ute
Melted eggs in the back of the ute
Uncle Les in a bunny suit
Uncle Les in a bunny suit
Sticky faces, choc delight
Sticky faces, choc delight
Better brush your teeth tonight!
Better brush your teeth tonight!

Chorus

Aunty Chris, the mother hen
Aunty Chris, the mother hen
Popped down for the long weekend
Popped down for the long weekend
Baskets full of Easter treats
Baskets full of Easter treats
Chicken slippers on her feet
Chicken slippers on her feet

Chorus

Easter Monday picnic trip
Easter Monday picnic trip
Family cricket, have a dip
Family cricket, have a dip
Head for home here comes the rain!
Head for home here comes the rain!
Let's get out the old board games . . .
Let's get out all the old board games . . .

Chorus

The Easter Long Weekend

Chorus
The Easter Long Weekend
Has rolled around again
It's a four day break—
You beauty, mate!
The Easter Long Weekend

The roads out of the city
Will be choked with cars and vans
It's an annual tradition—
The Easter traffic jam
It's fish and chips to take away
Unpack the camping gear
Enjoy the peace and quiet
Cos the phones don't work out here

Chorus

There'll be lots and lots of fishing
I'll tell you that for free
From beaches, boats and headlands
In lakes and mountain streams
There'll be houseboats on the rivers
They'll be sailing on the bay
And if the surf is any good
They'll carve it up all day

Chorus

There are tents among the blue gums
Campfires and guitars
As the sparks go curling upwards
To get lost among the stars
And the kookaburras cackle
In the early morning glow
It's an Easter Sunday sunrise
And there's still two days to go!

Chorus

When it's Easter in Australia

Chorus
When it's Easter in Australia
Everywhere you go
There are cavalcades and carnivals
Shindigs and shows
Aussies love a party
And if the weather's fine
There'll be markets, fetes and festivals
At Easter time

It's blues up in Byron
And jazz in Wollongong
Gospel in Toowoomba
Darwin's rockin' on
Opera in the outback
Classics by the sea
And the marching bands in Nambour
All go 1 – 2 – 3!

Chorus

There are motorbikes in Bathurst
The Boulia Rodeo
There's steam trains on the Bellarine
Parades in Bendigo
It's the William Creek Gymkhana
A feast in Innisfail
And there's bargains at the Little Hampton
Car Boot Sale

Chorus

Little Barry Bilby

Little Barry Bilby had a fly upon his nose
Little Barry Bilby had a fly upon his nose
Little Barry Bilby had a fly upon his nose
So he flipped it and he flapped it
And it flew away

Poor little Barry Bilby
Poor little Barry Bilby
Poor little Barry Bilby
So he flipped it and he flapped it
And it flew away

The Easter Hat Parade

Chorus
Hey! Ho!
What a show!
Look at what we made
As we go marching round and round
In the Easter Hat Parade

A silver outer space hat
Ones with lots of leaves
Colourful hats with ribbons
Blowing in the breeze

Chorus

Spots and stripes and pom poms
Feathers on the top
A bouncy big balloony hat
I hope it doesn't pop

Chorus

Crazy hats with doodahs
That reach down to the floor
It's an Easter Bonnet Brouhaha
Easter hats galore!

Hey! Ho!
What a show!
Look at what we made
As we go marching round and round
In the Easter Hat Parade
As we go marching round and round
We go marching round and round
We go marching round and round
In the Easter Hat Parade

The Great Big Aussie Easter Egg Hunt

Chorus
It's Easter time in Australia mate
And we're searching high and low
It's the Great Big Aussie Easter Egg Hunt
Get ready
Get set
And go!

We found some out near Uluru
As the sun was going down
And in Alice Springs it didn't take us long
To bag a few in town
We got some up the Katherine Gorge
As we paddled our canoe
And the thunder roared
As we found some more
On the road to Kakadu

Chorus

And up on Thursday Island
We picked up one or two
And we spotted some in the Daintree
As the crocs were floating through
We snagged a few in Adelaide
Down on Rundle Mall
And two or three
At the MCG
We thought were footy balls!

Chorus

The Tassie devils helped us
The fairy penguins, too
And old mate Bilby lent a hand
And cousin Kangaroo
We found plenty in the outback
With the clapstick and the didj
And we found a whole lot
At the very very top
Of the Sydney Harbour Bridge!

Chorus

Australians All Love Hot Cross Buns

Australians all love hot cross buns
At Easter they are beaut
Thirteen to a dozen filled
With little chunks of fruit
And when it comes to Easter eggs
The buns are best by far
Cos hot cross buns won't melt or spoil
When you leave them in the car

Australians know the hot cross buns
A classic recipe
That cannot be improved upon
In any bakery
For when they chuck in chocolate chips
And sprinkly bits they fail
Those naughty bakers should be sent
To naughty baker jail

Australians love a hot cross bun
So bunny, crossed and hot
By countless millions every year
We'll gobble up the lot
You spot them early January
On to the shelves they come
An Aussie Easter's three months long
Thanks to the hot cross bun
With flour and fruit and cinna-mun
We love a hot cross bun!

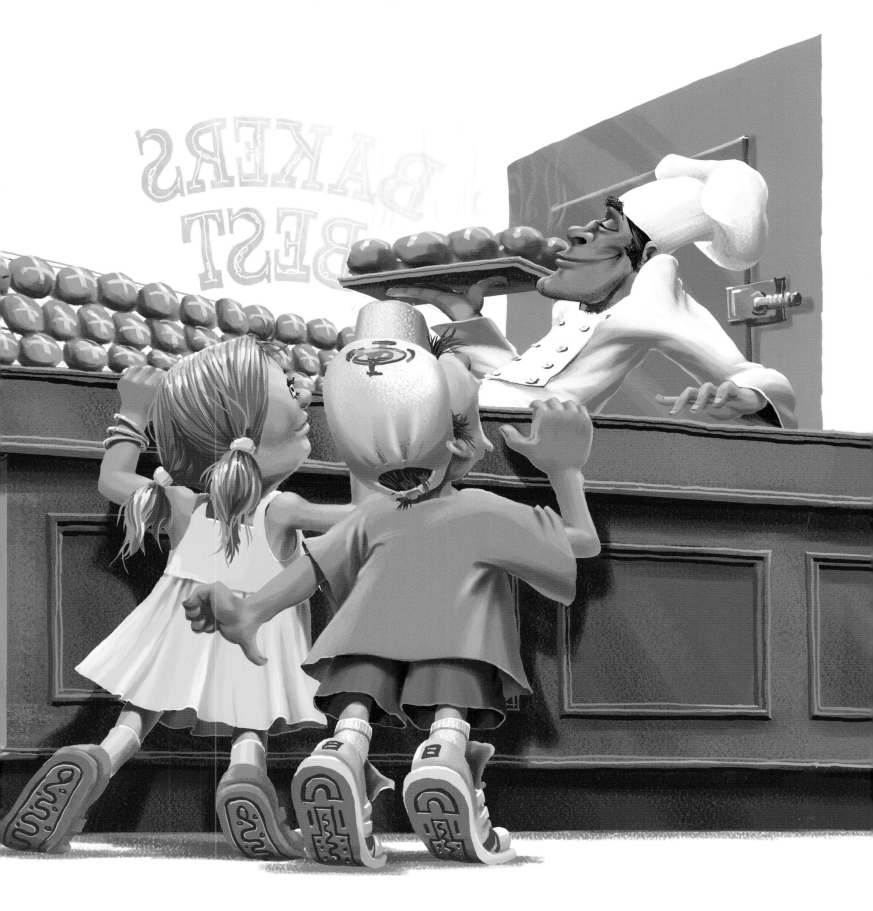

The Easter Bunny Got the Sack

Once the Easter Bunny
Got the call to Canberra
That's when they told him
Don't come back
Cos Australia needs
An Aussie Easter animal
And that's how the Easter Bunny
Got the sack

Chorus
Easter koala
Easter goanna
Easter wombat
Easter kangaroo
Bilby, bogi
All of 'em are dinky di
This Aussie Easter'll
Be true blue

Well the word spread quickly
On the old bush telegraph
To every billabong and old gum tree
Aussie animals
Native to Australia
Were asking the question
'Will they pick me?'

Chorus

Back in Canberra
A mob of Aussie animals
Marched on the parliament
In one big line . . .
And no-one could agree
Till down came the prime minister
'Youse can ALL have the job
This Easter time!'

Easter koalas
Easter goannas
Easter wombats
Easter kangaroos
Bilbys, bogis
All of 'em are dinky di
This Aussie Easter'll
Be true blue!